MICHAEL PAYNE

Beyond the Commit

The Human Side of Software Development

This book was professionally typeset on Reedsy.
Find out more at reedsy.com

For those who taught me, challenged me, encouraged me to keep asking questions, and reminded me not to take myself too seriously.

"Always pass on what you have learned."

— Yoda, Return of the Jedi

Contents

Acknowledgments

This book didn't happen in a vacuum. I've been lucky enough to have teachers, peers, students, and leaders whose voices still echo in my work—and in my head—long after the meetings ended and the projects shipped.

To my mentors—Michael Payne Sr., Steve Helms, Arnie Maslow, and Bob Mills—thank you for teaching me to pause before acting. Arnie and Bob are no longer with us, but the lessons they left me still feel fresh: slow down, think it through, and never confuse movement for progress.

To my peers—Ian Wright, Jed Racine, Jared Coleson, Chad Yates, Bryan Rojo, and TJ Sutton—thank you for pushing me, challenging me, and never letting me settle for "good enough." You've each sharpened my thinking in ways that made the work better and made me better in the process.

To my students—Brandon Swenson, Bill Swartwood, and Bryan Beale—watching Brandon and Bill grow has been a reminder that learning is never one-way, and it never really ends. Bryan, who we lost to Non-Hodgkin's Lymphoma, left behind a presence I still miss to this day. His curiosity, humor, and kindness are woven into the fabric of this work.

To the leaders who encouraged me to keep asking questions—Linda Brooks-Rix, James Miller, John Marhefka, and Matt Buckleman—thank you for making curiosity not just safe, but valued. That trust gave me the room to explore, to experiment, and to fail forward.

And finally, to Liz, Ryleigh, Cohen, Andrew, and Graham—you've given me the best lesson of all: not to take myself so dang seriously. You've kept me grounded in the messy, wonderful reality outside the keyboard, and I'm endlessly grateful for it.

I

The Way of the Coder

The seasoned developer learns to let go: of control, of ego, of needing to be right. Tools are transient. Titles change. Systems fade. What matters is focus, awareness, and the ability to act without attachment. This is the quiet strength behind lasting code.

1

Starting with Stillness

"When the mind is nowhere, it is everywhere."
— Takuan Sōhō, *The Unfettered Mind*

When you start a new task or project, how quickly are your fingers on the keyboard? I'd bet it's minutes—maybe seconds. There are deadlines, urgent bugs, and a constant push to deliver. Even with AI assistants ready to generate code, the pressure to produce remains.

Stillness isn't about sitting cross-legged in silence. It's about returning your attention to the moment. In that stillness, clarity rises.

I'm sure most developers have felt that jolt of release anxiety. It gets worse when the release includes bugs. Your job feels like it's on the line, and your nervous system reacts accordingly.

I once got a bug report over Slack for a feature I'd shipped earlier that day. I'd been bracing for something to go wrong. Before anyone added more detail to the thread, my brain had already decided: this was critical. I dove into the code, scanning for potential causes. Suddenly, everything looked unfamiliar and suspicious.

Meanwhile, people were still posting in the thread. When I finally paused to read the full conversation, it became obvious: it wasn't a code issue. It was a configuration error.

If I'd responded with awareness instead of reacting out of fear, I would've saved myself a lot of energy, stress, and time.

Urgency clouds perception. I didn't used to question it. I just obeyed it. But whatever created that urgency was also controlling my behavior - and undermining my effectiveness.

I would move faster and see less.

Eventually, I couldn't keep up with every new fire, every demand, every ping. In tech, instant gratification isn't just baked into the product; It's baked into the process. So slowing down feels unnatural.

But attention isn't reactive. It's receptive. And that shift—from reacting to responding—is a change in posture that changes everything.

Stillness doesn't require hours of meditation. Just a breath. Just a pause.

Practice: Myself before My Code

Try this:

- Before jumping into code, pause for one full breath.
- Read the message or bug report twice before responding.
- Name what's driving your urgency—then **ask** if it's true.

Small shifts in attention create space for better decisions. Especially when the pressure is loud.

You don't have to respond immediately. You don't even have to understand everything at once. You just have to pause long enough to notice what's actually in front of you.

Before you write code, calm the coder.

2

Read Code like a Story

The first thing I do when I open a codebase is read. I'm not skimming for function names or searching for a bug. I'm reading like I'm joining a conversation that's already in progress. I want to understand the tone, the shortcuts, the patterns, the seams.

Because if you don't know what story the code is already telling, you're not continuing it. You're interrupting it.

One of my earliest mentors, Arnie Maslow, was the kind of developer who had no reason to help a couple of local teenagers learn to code. But he did. He took us seriously before we had any idea what we were doing.

One day, I couldn't get my code to behave. I asked Arnie for help. He ran it, looked at me, and asked, "What's it supposed to do?"

I stumbled. I wasn't describing what it *should* do. I was describing what I *thought* it was doing.

Frustrated, I speculated that I might have found a bug in the .NET Framework.

Arnie chuckled. "The computer only does what you tell it to do. Nothing more."

He was right. I had to go back and read the code—again and again—until I finally understood what it was actually doing. Only then could I change it. That moment stuck with me.

Reading code isn't something you outgrow. It's the most fundamental aspect of software development. And one of the easiest to skip.

I get asked all the time, "How do I get better at coding?" My first question is usually, "What code have you read today?"

Most people stop there. Because the answer is often: none.

Reading code (especially code you didn't write) takes effort. It asks you to set aside assumptions, ego, and urgency - and just listen. To observe. To understand what the code is trying to do, and what problem it was written to solve.

And that's the beginning of real growth.

Takeaway: Always be Reading

If you want to grow as a developer, read code every day.

- Read outside your own commits.

- Read code that confuses you—twice.
- Read with curiosity, not judgment.

And when you think you understand it, explain it out loud. If you can't, you don't.

We don't always inherit clean code. But we always inherit a story. Every system carries memory: of trade-offs, urgency, and forgotten plans.

To shape it well, you have to listen first.

The code speaks. Are you listening?

3

Clarity is Kindness - Especially in Code

"Truth is ever to be found in simplicity, and not in the multiplicity and confusion of things."
—Isaac Newton

Have you ever tried to get your pet to look at something, and when you point, all they do is stare at your finger? The act of pointing only makes sense if it's paired with meaning—like saying, *"Look at that."*

Our industry does this same dance with mantras like "clean coding." The blog post, the book, the talk—they're pointing at something important. But too often, we get fixated on the finger

So let's name it clearly. Clean coding is a decision to make life easier for someone else. Maybe for your teammate. Maybe for your future self.

Clarity isn't just more elegant than cleverness—it's empathy.

Even as an experienced developer, I've fallen into the trap of trying to be clever with naming. On one project, I was building a configuration management system. I spent an embarrassing amount of time trying to find the perfect "base name" for the class that would serve as the entry point for configuration values.

I settled on **Codex**. (It beat out **Grimoire**.) I have a bit of a penchant for magic.

From there, things spiraled. I named different configuration layers things like **CodexFundamentium** for reading environment variables. I even added some extension methods to the API startup pipeline with names like **AccioSettings**.

It was fun—for a while. But fun doesn't always age well in a codebase.

Eventually, it all started to feel like a riddle. The cleverness wore off, and what was left wasn't whimsical—it was hard to maintain. At that point, it wasn't just unhelpful. It was selfish. Or at the very least, short on empathy.

Naming things is hard. It always has been. But trying to be clever makes it harder—for everyone else. When we prioritize creativity over clarity, we create code that feels like an inside joke. The problem is, the audience keeps changing.

What makes perfect sense in the moment may feel like a mystery six months later—even to you. And for the person who didn't sit through your brainstorming session or doesn't share your taste in metaphors, cleverness becomes a burden.

Clarity, on the other hand, is universal. It doesn't rely on context, shared humor, or cultural references. It's a signal that you're not just writing code to get something working—you're writing it for the person who comes after. And that's the heart of the craft.

Takeaway: Clear Coding

Every name you write—class, method, or variable—is a sentence fragment in someone else's mental conversation.

- Be descriptive, not clever.
- Be boring, if it helps clarity.
- Favor obvious over original.
- Refactor names when their meaning changes.

The reader isn't your audience. The reader *is you*, just a little further down the road.

The best code doesn't need to impress. It guides.

If your cleverness gets in the way of someone else's understanding, you're pointing at your finger—not the moon.

To write clearly is to care for the reader.

4

Before AI - Read Code, Review Code. After AI - Read Code, Review Code

There's a certain wonder the first time you watch an AI assistant generate a complete chunk of code. But that wonder fades quickly when you realize: it's not magic. It's just prediction.

The AI will give you answers. Confidently. But confidence isn't correctness.

There's a natural desire to trust it. I see that same instinct in less experienced colleagues: the code runs, so it must be good. But the discipline of software engineering—whether you're working alone or in a team—is to review that work with care. And when it comes from AI, maybe even more so.

I've been mentoring developers for more than a decade, and one thing hasn't changed—most early-career devs are eager to level up as quickly as possible. The question comes up often: "How do I get better at this?"

My answer has always been the same: *Read more code.* Read your own. Read mine. Read the open source libraries you're using. Read it all.

There's a moment in *Doctor Strange* that captures this idea well. Stephen is confronting the Ancient One, still looking for a shortcut to healing his hands. It's dawning on him that what he's being asked to learn isn't science—it's magic.

> **The Ancient One:** *"How did you get to reattach severed nerves and put a human spine back together, bone by bone?"*
> **Doctor Strange:** *"Study and practice. Years of it."*

All real crafts are like that: study and practice, side by side. Yet in tech, we tend to focus on the practice and skip the study.

But with AI coding assistants becoming part of everyday development, the study part is more important than ever. When you're not the one writing every line, reading becomes the craft.

There's a lot of excitement—and a fair amount of concern—about the rise of "vibe coding." So let's be clear: vibe coding is completely devoid of the core skill at the heart of software engineering—understanding code.

The moment you apply foundational principles like design patterns or clean code, you're invoking a level of understanding that current AI tools can't replicate. And once you do that, it's no longer vibe coding. It's something more deliberate: a collaboration between human judgment and machine-generated utility.

But that only works if you're reading. You can't review what you don't understand. And you can't understand what you haven't read.

If you're vibe coding without reviewing, you're not writing software—you're throwing dice.

Practice: Reviewing Code

If AI wrote the code, review it like a teammate handed it to you.

- Read it top to bottom.
- Say out loud what it's supposed to do.
- Ask what it *assumes* is true.
- Ask what it breaks if it's wrong.
- Run it. Test it. Read it again. Repeat.

Don't trust the confidence. Trust the review.

AI might change the way we write. But it doesn't change who we are when we sit with the code.

The tools evolve. The attention remains.

5

Unattached to the Outcome. Focused on the Process

"Fall in love with the process, and the results will come."
— Eric Thomas

Some of the hardest moments in my career came when I did everything right—and the project still missed the mark.

The deadline slipped. The client changed direction. A feature I'd poured myself into got cut at the last minute or rewritten by someone else. And suddenly, all the late nights, the careful planning, the clean code—it felt pointless.

It's easy, in moments like that, to start measuring your worth by the outcome. To think that if it didn't ship, or didn't get noticed, or didn't go perfectly, then you failed.

But that's not the point.

The point is that you showed up with intention. You practiced the craft. You communicated clearly. You built something that could stand on its own—even if it didn't get the spotlight.

The outcome matters. But your peace can't depend on it.

There was a time when I tied my self-worth to the success of every project. If the sprint went well, I felt like a genius. If a deadline slipped, or the feature got cut, or leadership changed direction, I took it personally—like I had failed.

That roller coaster worked for a while. I was productive. I was proud. I was also exhausted.

Eventually, I hit a wall. The volatility of outcomes—many of which I couldn't control—started to erode my energy and my confidence. I'd find myself holding onto decisions that were already out of my hands, trying to rewrite the outcome in my head.

I had to relearn how to work.

I had to shift my focus to the process itself—how I communicated, how I built, how I cared for the code and the people around me. That became the measure of success. Not the Jira ticket. Not the launch. Not the applause.

Just the craft. Just the presence. Just the practice.

When your sense of progress is tied only to outcomes, you'll burn out. And when your sense of accomplishment is tied only to outcomes, you'll start to feel like an imposter. There aren't many positive effects that come from being attached to the end result.

But the answer isn't to *detach* from the outcome either. To detach is to become apathetic—to stop caring about the work itself—and that's not the goal. Instead, imagine holding the outcome loosely in your hand, allowing it to change or even slip away if it needs to. This is what we call *non-attachment.*

Features get cut. Priorities shift. Definitions of success change mid-sprint. Sometimes the best work gets discarded, and other times rushed code gets celebrated because it shipped on time. You can't control all of that.

What you can control is how you show up. The deeper craft lives in your consistency, your care, and how you communicate— regardless of how the story ends.

The real story is how you move through the work, and how present you are in each moment along the way.

Practice: Holding without Holding On

Try this when things feel uncertain:

- Name one part of the work you can fully control today.
- Focus on quality, communication, and presence in that task.
- Acknowledge the outcome, then loosen your grip.
- End the day asking how you *showed up*, not what shipped.

Peace comes from participation, not prediction.

Outcomes drift. Recognition fades.

But presence leaves a longer trace—on the code, on the team, and on you. Practice is the part you keep.

The build may fail. The practice continues.

II

The Tools are not The Path

A new framework won't fix your burnout. A design pattern won't save your project. And no, renaming that one variable for the fifth time won't make you a better person. Tools are fun. Shiny, even. But they're not the path. The path is learning to think clearly while surrounded by chaos... and semicolons.

6

If You Find the Perfect Framework, Abandon It

The first time you use a new framework, it feels like falling in love. The code flows. The architecture makes sense. Everything just clicks. It's almost like the framework's creator understands exactly how you think about code—which, of course, is the right way to think about code.

But eventually, it breaks your heart. The magic fades. You start running into edge cases, workarounds, undocumented limitations. That elegant abstraction starts to leak. And you realize—you weren't seeing the framework clearly; you were projecting.

We fall into the trap of confirmation bias. We notice every feature that confirms our belief that we've found "the one," and ignore every warning sign that says otherwise.

It wasn't perfect. It was just new. You weren't in love. You were in lust.

A leaky abstraction is one that hides complexity—but not completely. The abstraction simplifies something for everyday use, but the underlying behavior still finds ways to show through. A classic example is SQL. At first glance, querying a database seems simple: just select what you want. But write the wrong kind of join, and suddenly you're dealing with a Cartesian Product that returns millions of rows and cripples performance. That's the leak.

In my view, all abstractions are leaky by nature. It's not a bug. It's the very nature of the thing.

The moment you create a layer that wraps complexity, you're also creating the potential for mismatch—between what you think you're hiding and what you're actually simplifying. The cracks are inevitable. It's a kind of software physics: a "you can't have your cake and eat it too" principle embedded in the structure of code.

Frameworks are just large-scale abstractions. They handle common cases, reduce boilerplate, and give you guardrails. But by doing that, they force decisions. They constrain you to their view of the world. Sooner or later, your problem won't fit that worldview. That's when the abstraction starts to leak—and the disappointment sets in.

Takeaway: *Recognizing the Truth*

True inventions, like HTTP, don't abstract so much as enable. They create entirely new spaces—new protocols, new metaphors, new tools—that other things can be built inside of. HTTP made the web. Frameworks make trade-offs.

The more we understand this, the more wisely we choose what to build on—and what to build ourselves.

- Don't mistake a framework for a philosophy.
- Frameworks are tools, not truths.
- Ask what the framework assumes, what it hides, and what it makes harder.
- Keep asking—even when it seems to be working.

When it stops working, don't fight it. Thank it—and move on.

Every framework feels perfect—until it doesn't. That's the nature of tools. They serve, then they strain. You weren't wrong to trust it. Just don't follow it off a cliff. And don't mistake the idea of perfection for the truth.

The perfect framework is an illusion.

7

Naming Things is Hard Because Thinking is Hard

"If you can't explain it simply, you don't understand it well enough."
— Albert Einstein

We joke that naming things is one of the hardest problems in computer science. But it's not really about the names. It's about understanding.

Naming forces us to confront the messiness in our thinking. It asks us to make a decision about what something *is*, not just what it does. That's hard—because, often, we don't fully know. We reach for vague terms, generic verbs, or clever phrasing to cover up the fact that our mental model isn't solid yet.

A poor name doesn't just make things harder to read. It cements confusion. It invites misunderstandings that ripple forward—until someone finally asks, "What is this actually doing?"

We've all seen it—and most of us have done it.

From the very beginning, we're taught programming through oversimplified examples like:

```
int add(int a, int b) {
  return a + b;
}
```

Sometimes even less helpful than that.

And when we're stuck and asking for help, we tend to reduce the problem down to the smallest possible unit—the isolated bug, the single method—so someone can help us solve it faster. What we get back is often code with vague function names, throwaway variable names, and no real context. And because it works, we copy and paste it into our project without another thought.

That's where the naming debt begins.

On top of that, modern languages have their own obstacles. Verbose syntax, long type declarations, and the trade-off between vertical and horizontal space all make naming harder to see—and easier to skip.

So now we've got two things working against us: we learned the craft in a world of contrived examples, and we work in environments that quietly discourage clarity.

We have every excuse not to name things well.

And every reason to stop and make sure we do.

When naming something feels hard, it's not a sign to move faster. It's a signal to slow down.

A vague name is often the first warning that we don't understand what the code is really doing—or what it should be doing. Good names don't just improve readability. They improve thinking. Naming is where design happens in miniature.

If you can't describe it clearly, you probably haven't seen it clearly. A confusing name is rarely just a naming problem. It's a thinking problem that hasn't been addressed yet.

Practice: Skillful Naming

When naming feels hard, stop writing and start describing.

- Say out loud what the thing does—or what it's supposed to do.
  (Be careful about semantic satiation. "Manager" will start to sound like a myth.)
- Ask what it would mean to someone reading this six months from now.
- If the name is still vague, the code probably needs to be split, simplified, or reconsidered.

Naming is a design step. Treat it with the same care you give to your architecture.

It's tempting to grab a name and move on. But a bad name is a bug in disguise.

Slow down. Listen to your code. Let it tell you what it wants to be called.

He who names well, sees clearly.

8

You Modernize Their Code. I Modernize Their Understanding.

Code doesn't appear out of nowhere. It reflects the people who wrote it—their priorities, their constraints, and most of all, their understanding. If you only change the code, you're treating the symptom, not the cause.

Take Angular, for example. It's been around for nearly 15 years. Version 1.0 saw wide adoption, and it was supported all the way through 2022. But when Angular 2.0 arrived in 2016, it broke everything. It wasn't just an update—it was a ground-up rewrite that required new tooling and a completely new way of thinking.

If you started learning Angular in version 14, you likely didn't experience that shift. You were native to the new paradigm. You may have heard that upgrading from version 1 was painful—but that's not the same as having your own mental model broken and rebuilt.

Each version of a framework comes with a set of assumptions. The longer you've worked with a tool, the more versions of it you've had to unlearn. And the further you've come, the more likely you are to call those mismatches "technical debt." But often, what we're really seeing isn't bad code. It's fossilized thinking.

When you modernize a codebase but keep the old mental models intact, all you're really doing is changing the wrappers. The real system—the one made of habits, assumptions, and mental shortcuts—stays the same.

You'll see the same shortcuts reappear, just in a shinier framework. You'll see architectural decisions made to mirror the past, not to serve the present. And eventually, you'll wonder why everything still feels hard, even after all that effort.

That's not just technical debt. That's **conceptual debt**. And no linter or upgrade guide is going to pay it off for you.

This is why so many government and financial systems written in FORTRAN or COBOL are still running today—and still *working*. Their logic was built to match a specific reality, and that reality is still shaping how those systems operate. Modernizing them isn't just about rewriting code. It's about rethinking the world they were designed to reflect.

Modernizing code is important. But modernizing *understanding* is essential.

Takeaway: Practical Assumption Elimination

Before you modernize:
Don't just ask "How is this built?"
Ask:

- "Why was it built this way?"
- "What assumptions shaped it?"
- "Who depends on it working like this?"
- "What problem are we still solving?"

You're not just updating code. You're inheriting a worldview.

While you modernize:
Document both what the system does *and* what it's trying to do. Capture technical structure—but also your understanding of each piece and how it fits into the larger purpose. This is not just for the next developer. It's for future you.

Work in the smallest meaningful units possible. Even if the goal is fast change, treat it like evolution.

Systems improve best one thoughtful step at a time.

You can modernize a codebase without ever modernizing the system. And you can modernize a system without ever modernizing the thinking. Real progress happens when all three evolve together.

The system is not the code. It is the thinking behind it.

30

9

Every Tool Introduces a New Kind of Pain

"All things are difficult before they are easy."
— Thomas Fuller

We choose tools to move faster, build better, or simplify complexity. And often, they deliver—especially at the beginning.

But every tool comes with its own shape. Its own assumptions. Its own new edge cases. You don't just gain capabilities— you inherit new constraints. Sometimes you solve the original problem and inherit three more in return.

That's not failure. That's the nature of tools.

I remember the first time I adopted an ORM. I was working in VB.NET—around the time .NET 3.5 was still new—and Entity Framework was either nonexistent or barely viable. I'd evaluated a few options and landed on NHibernate for a desktop app I was maintaining. I wanted two things: cleaner data access, and the ability to use LINQ. Fortunately, someone had built a LINQ-to-NHibernate extension.

I thought this would solve one of our core problems: the mystery of where every reference to a column, table, or stored procedure was hiding in the codebase. We'd had too many releases with silent breakages after a database change. An ORM, I figured, would give us traceability and structure.

And it did—sort of.

Stored procedures weren't well-supported, and our system depended heavily on them. That friction was manageable. But then came a bug that took me three days to track down. A specific LINQ query was returning no results. But if I ran the same logic directly in SQL? Perfectly fine.

I dove into the LINQ-to-NHibernate code. I downloaded the source, referenced the project locally, and started debugging line by line. It was some of the most confusing code I'd ever read. If not for the comments—mercifully explaining things like the Visitor Pattern—I would've been lost. I had to teach myself design patterns just to follow what was happening.

Three days later, I found it: a subtle mismatch in how VB.NET compiled expression trees, particularly around string comparisons, versus how NHibernate's C# internals interpreted them.

The ORM *did* help with many problems. But it didn't erase the pain—it just shifted it. The bugs were in a new place. The complexity moved one layer down. And the learning curve came with interest.

Every tool introduces a new kind of pain. That's not a failure. That's the trade.

You're always choosing which discomfort you'd rather live with:

- Do you want to hand-write SQL, or debug generated queries?
- Do you want full control, or better guardrails?
- Do you want more power, or more simplicity?

The problems never disappear—they just migrate.

The only mistake is thinking you've finally escaped them.

Practice: Choosing Wisely

Before adopting a tool, ask:

- What pain does this solve?
- What pain does this *introduce*?
- Do we understand the trade-offs, or are we being sold?

While using a tool, observe:

- Where are we struggling now?
- Are we solving the right problem—or just shifting the symptoms?

Tools don't remove pain. They repackage it.

Choose the trade with intention.

There's always a cost. Every tool, every fix, every abstraction—each one shifts the pain, not erases it. You can spend your time trying to avoid that cost, or you can learn to spend it well. Know what you're solving. Know what you're trading. Know what you're carrying forward.

To fix one thing is to break another. Choose the breakage mindfully.

10

A Pattern is Not a Practice

It's easy to fall in love with patterns. They're elegant. They're named. They make you feel like you're doing it right.

But design patterns aren't turn-key solutions. They're not magic recipes for scalable systems. Like the Pirate's Code, they're more guidelines than actual rules.

It's tempting to believe that if you just combine the right patterns, your system will build itself. Or that one pattern, applied precisely, can fix everything. But a pattern isn't a solution. It's a starting point. It's a suggestion—a shape you still have to understand, challenge, and adapt to.

A pattern is not the practice. The practice is how you wield it.

Most developers have lived through some form of this: a team or organization hears about a "best practice" and adopts it like gospel. The microservice pattern is one of the clearest examples.

It sounds clean in theory—small, focused services that can be deployed independently. But the pattern is intentionally vague about how *small* is "small." It doesn't dictate how many endpoints a service should have. It doesn't say whether a service should map to a bounded context, a business domain, or just a CRUD table. It leaves room for interpretation—because the pattern is about purpose, not prescription.

But instead of embracing that flexibility, many teams turn the pattern into a rulebook. Every microservice must have exactly one endpoint. Every team owns exactly one microservice. Every service must talk to every other service through a message bus— even when a shared library would be more appropriate. The result isn't better architecture. It's just more moving parts, glued together by dogma.

And it's not just code. Agile itself started as a set of values and principles—four core values, twelve simple ideas. But over time, those ideas were formalized into processes: Scrum, XP, SAFe. Some of them are useful. Some of them are not. But every one is just an implementation of the original pattern.

When you forget that, the practice becomes a ritual. You're standing up every day at 9am because the pattern said to— whether or not it helps anyone.

A pattern isn't sacred. It's a tool. And if you stop thinking, it will gladly think for you.

There's some irony in defining a principle here—after spending the chapter pointing out the limits of patterns.

But that's the point.

A pattern is only useful if you understand its purpose. If you can explain what it's for, when to apply it, and when to leave it behind, then it becomes a powerful tool. If you're just repeating what you've seen elsewhere, it's cargo cult programming—habits without clarity.

Design patterns aren't solutions. They're descriptions. They help us talk about code. They give us shared vocabulary. But applying one doesn't mean the job is done.

The real pattern to follow is this: think clearly, act intentionally, and don't mistake structure for substance.

Practice: Skillful Problem Solving

When reaching for a pattern, ask:

- What specific problem am I solving?
- Why does this pattern fit *this* situation?
- What trade-offs does it introduce?
- Could I explain this choice to a peer—without using the pattern's name?

Patterns are helpful. But your job isn't to implement them—it's to solve problems.

Practice means applying judgment, not just structure.

Patterns are useful. But only when you think with them—not through them.

You don't build better systems by following instructions. You build them by practicing awareness, context, and care.

Patterns don't solve problems. Practice does.

III

Leadership Without Control

True leadership isn't about control. It's about clarity, presence, and courage. The best leaders don't tighten their grip—they create space. They name what others avoid. They guide without ego. And when things go wrong, they respond with steady hands, not noise. In software and in life, real leadership shows up when we stop trying to dominate—and start learning how to hold without holding on.

11

Guide Without Gripping

"Be curious, not judgmental."
— Walt Whitman

As someone who's worked in corporate America for over 25 years, I understand why so much of our pop culture comedy about work hits home. The absurdity of office life—the status meetings, the leadership clichés, the performative urgency— it's all satire wrapped in truth. And while we in tech like to believe we've escaped it, we haven't. Sometimes our version of dysfunction just wears a hoodie and calls itself agile.

Leadership in IT often mirrors the leadership style of the broader business. That makes sense, especially when tech serves a non-tech organization. Structure cascades downward, and so does culture. Managers are often asked to "own their outcomes," but without training or intention, they just copy the behavior of the people above them. Control flows downhill.

So what do we get? Obsession with assigning tickets. Constant time tracking. A relentless need to prove we're working. All the little rituals that exist not to support the people doing the work, but to let someone else *cover their ass.*

But sometimes a person—or a company—breaks the cycle. And you begin to see that leadership isn't control. It's care. It's creating space, not filling it with noise. It's empowering the people doing the work, not breathing down their necks while they do it.

If you've ever cooked—or watched enough Gordon Ramsay— you know not to crowd the pan. If you jam too many steaks in at once, nothing cooks evenly. The heat drops. Things steam instead of sear. And there's no room left to move. That's what most corporate structures do. They crowd the pan.

The best leaders I've had didn't micromanage. They gave me room to push my own limits—and sometimes theirs. They let me fail, encouraged me to reflect, and asked better questions instead of giving tighter answers. They guided without gripping.

And I still remember them clearly—because they didn't have to shout to be heard.

My first "real" job was in IT support at the corporate head-quarters of a company in New Jersey. I was 15. It wasn't an internship in the traditional sense—I got the role because my dad also worked in IT there, as an AS/400 developer. My boss, Steve, ran the small desktop support team. He was quiet, blunt, and sharp as hell. Funny when he wanted to be. The kind of person who didn't need to say much to make an impression.

That summer, Steve gave me the chance to write real code. I was tasked with building an in-office chat system, inspired by AOL Instant Messenger. It was VB6 and SQL Server 6.5, and I was working from old MSDN CDs and printed manuals. I ran into problems, like trying to get the window to flash when a message arrived. I crashed the IDE repeatedly. I asked Steve for help, and he gave suggestions—but not solutions. He let me find my way. And I did.

At the end of the summer, he gave me a short review I'll never forget:

> "You're not afraid to try things most programmers three times your age wouldn't touch with a ten-foot pole. I admire that. Keep it."

I did. And I still do.

Fast-forward a few years to a very different experience. I was working for a company led by someone I'll call Jon Doe. I don't use his real name, not out of disrespect, but because what I learned is more important than who taught me.

Jon wasn't a developer. He was an entrepreneur who built a SaaS business before "SaaS" was even a thing. I started in support and was quickly promoted—within three months I was leading a key project, chosen over others with more experience and degrees.

But the culture was... rigid. Every task lived inside a ticketing system with time tracking. Every decision had to go through

Jon. Even when I proposed better ways to solve problems—and even when those ideas were accepted—he wanted to be part of every call, every step, every checkbox. His face would turn red when I asked too many questions. He said it was acid reflux. I suspect I caused some of it.

I'm resilient. Some might say stubborn. I stayed five years. I built things I'm proud of. But I couldn't change the culture. The pan was too crowded. Everyone was cooking to avoid scrutiny—not to create anything great.

Eventually, I realized what I was: a big fish in a small pond, swimming in circles. I needed more space. A bigger team. A place where leaders made room, not noise.

And that made all the difference.

The strongest leadership doesn't come from control. It comes from trust, clarity, and presence.

You can assign work without assigning meaning, and you can track time without understanding value. But if your team is optimizing for your comfort instead of the customer's need, you're not leading—you're managing anxiety.

Leadership is about clearing space, not crowding it. Creating the kind of room where someone else can try, stretch, and sometimes fail. The kind of room where their thinking matters more than your ego.

Micromanagement is not accountability. It's just control with a spreadsheet.

The pattern is simple: guide without gripping. Be visible. Be present. But don't block the heat.

Practice: Modeling Good Leadership

If you're in a leadership role:

- Create space. Ask questions that open thought, not control outcomes.
- Don't measure trust in hours. Measure it in how freely your team shares problems and ideas.
- Leave room for failure—and reflection.

If you're not in a leadership role (yet):

- Model the kind of leadership you wish you had.
- Ask better questions. Share what you've learned. Encourage others to try.
- Be someone who clears space, even without authority.

The best guidance creates possibility—not pressure.

Lead by lighting the path, not standing in the way.

You don't have to push to lead. You don't have to pull, either. You just have to walk clearly enough that others can see the way.

In Chapter 5, we explored the idea of practicing non-attachment to outcome. *Guide Without Gripping* is a continuation of that practice. The toxic environments we've all experienced are born from attachment—control, fear, ego. But when you release your grip on the outcome and hold it gently, you create space. Space for others to grow. Space for the work to breathe. Space for change, because everything changes.

To lead is not to hold.

It is to open the path.

12

Code Review is a Conversation, Not a Performance

I think—though I don't know for sure—that when the practice of code review entered our industry, it brought with it a little corporate baggage. A bit of performance culture. A bit of fear.

It's built into our tools. Pull requests have *Approvers*. They get *Approved* or *Rejected*. You can require a quorum of approvers before merging. The language itself—reject, approve, required—carries a subtle but powerful message: *someone is above you in this decision.*

And maybe that's why code review can feel loaded. I find myself hesitating over who to add as a reviewer—not because I need feedback, but because I'm looking for someone with *authority*. And often, I don't have a clear authority. I just have peers. But the tool doesn't speak in the language of peers. It speaks in the language of judgment.

When we enter reviews with that mindset, everything becomes

performative. The code is the performance. Every comment becomes critique. The ego steps up, ready to defend—and now I have to burn even more energy just trying to keep it in check. Because I know ...professionally, emotionally, and practically... that's not what review is for.

Maybe it's just semantics. But maybe it's not.

What if the button didn't say "Approve"—what if it said "Understood"?
What if instead of "Reject," it said "Needs Clarity"?
What if we replaced "Reviewers" with "Cohorts"?

Would that shift our posture? Would we stop trying to be right and start trying to connect? Would it feel less like a critique and more like a conversation?

And wouldn't that be the point?

I have to admit: I've been on both sides of this.

I've been the person who took every comment on a pull request as a judgment. And I've also been the reviewer who left those comments without enough care. It wasn't until the idea for this chapter hit me that I really stepped back and started to question the way we treat code review—not just culturally, but personally.

Not long ago, I submitted a large PR for a major feature. It was a meaningful chunk of work that I needed to get merged and released. At the same time, the company had just hired a new senior director over infrastructure—someone I didn't know yet, but who clearly had authority above mine, at least in the org chart. I submitted the PR. And then the comments started.

My email lit up. One comment after another. Some were on code I hadn't even touched. I could feel my anxiety rising with every ping.

I talked to my direct manager about it, trying to make sense of it. Eventually I set up a conversation with the new director himself. And it turned out... he wasn't judging my work at all. He was just trying to understand the codebase. The comments weren't critiques. They were clarifying questions. The disconnect wasn't in his intention—it was in my perception.

I was feeling exposed. Evaluated. Like I was being graded.

Because that's what the tool and the process had trained me to expect.

And I've been on the other side, too. I once mentored and employed a junior developer just starting their career. They submitted a PR, and I—stressed, tired, ego high—left comments that weren't curious or kind. I told them how I would've done it. I dismissed their thinking instead of inviting them to share more. It wasn't thoughtful. It was performative. And I regret it.

There's a deeper cultural current here too. A kind of inherited hazing.

New developers are often thrown into the lion's den of cynical, burned-out seniors who haven't touched grass in 20 years. The expectation is that you "earn your place" through critique and silence. Through holding your tongue and toughening your skin.

It's toxic. It's trauma. It's unnecessary.

Code review can be a conversation. It should be a conversation. But only if we're willing to stop performing and start listening.

Code review is not a final exam. It's not a performance review.

It's a place where people meet to share thinking and make things better—together. The strongest pattern for healthy review isn't technical. It's relational.

Lead with curiosity. Ask before correcting. Assume good intent.

If you don't understand something, say so. "Tell me more" is always a stronger move than "This is wrong."

Good review culture is built on small behaviors:

- Use questions more than statements.
- Reflect tone back—never escalate it.
- Let go of proving. Focus on improving.

If the goal is better code, then the practice is better conversation.

Practice: Skillful Code Reviews

When reviewing code:

- Lead with questions: *"Can you walk me through this part?"*
- Avoid loaded words like *"should"* or *"obviously."*
- Praise what works—don't just fix what's broken.
- If something's unclear, ask *"Can we clarify this?"* instead of *"This is confusing."*

When receiving review:

- Don't assume tone from text—clarify before reacting.
- Ask reviewers to explain their reasoning, not just their reaction.
- Remember: your work is not your worth.

The best reviews aren't about being right. They're about being real—with each other, and with the work.

If your goal is to communicate, which would you prefer?

Sharing a quiet table at a restaurant with soft music and open conversation? Or shouting over the noise in a crowded bar, straining to be heard?

Most of us would choose the former. Code review is the same.

When a review becomes about proving something, nobody grows—we're too busy trying to talk over the noise.

But when it becomes a conversation—quiet, curious, and clear—everyone grows.

If the review is loud, the learning is silent.

13

Strong Opinions, Loosely Held — Until Tested

"You're welcome to test that assumption at your convenience."
— Captain Jean Luc Picard, Star Trek: The Next Generation

We are trained—by our jobs, our education, and especially our culture—to value certainty. Or more specifically, to value *binary thinking.*

If it's not this, it must be that. If you're not with me, you're against me. If it's not right, it must be wrong.

But not everything in life—or in code—fits into a binary. Many of the concepts our culture is currently wrestling with are spectrum-based:

Sexuality, identity, neurodivergence.

It's messy. It's uncomfortable. And it's freeing.

The more tightly we cling to binary models, the more mental effort we waste trying to force the world into neat little boxes. That effort isn't neutral—it costs us. It becomes a kind of cognitive bloat. A bug in the way we think.

And we carry those bugs with us—into our work, into our teams, into our code.

We stop questioning assumptions.
We stop saying "I don't know."
We build around belief instead of truth.

This isn't a call to abandon strong opinions. It's a reminder that *strong* doesn't have to mean *immovable*. You can say "I'm sure," and still be ready to say "I was wrong." You can believe something deeply—and let it go when it's tested.

The moment you grip too tightly, you stop learning.

This story isn't directly about code—but it might be one of the most important lessons I've ever learned about attachment to belief.

At one job, I spent a lot of time simply observing how things worked. I'd been taught that understanding group dynamics at a company's headquarters was key to being effective—not just politically, but practically. Navigate personalities, improve process, and you could create real wins for your career *and* your team.

In this case, my boss—our team lead—was getting overwhelmed with direct communication from the help desk. The structure was simple: tier-one help desk handled support for both hardware and internal corporate software. But when a ticket involved our custom applications and the help desk person didn't know what to do, they forwarded it straight to the lead developer. Constantly.

That seemed... inefficient. A poor use of time. I started thinking about better documentation, but we didn't have the tech writing bandwidth for what was really needed. Then something unexpected happened: the big boss decided one of our developers—a guy who wasn't particularly strong, struggled with bugs and release anxiety—should be let go. It was almost Christmas. My boss brought it to me, and I said flat-out, *"I'm not firing someone right before the holidays. There has to be another way."*

That's when something clicked.

I proposed creating a second-tier help desk role—someone who'd catch and triage these escalated tickets *before* they hit the team leads. And I proposed that the struggling developer take that role instead of being fired.

It sounded simple. It wasn't.

That proposal kicked off two weeks of meetings, debates, and pushback across software, hardware, and even the training department. At one point, the big boss—clearly frustrated— gathered everyone and said, *"This position is redundant. The help desk already does this."*

I replied, *"If the help desk is doing it, why are the emails still going to the team leads?"*

That didn't land well.

He fired back, *"If you're not going to be part of the solution, you can get out of this office."*

I shut my mouth. I let it go. And we moved forward with the plan—on a trial basis.

Thirty days in, the big boss said, *"It's going okay. I'm still not sure, but we'll continue."*
Sixty days in—I wasn't there.
But at ninety days, the same person who pushed back so hard sat in a meeting and said:
"I can't imagine how we ever did it without this position. This was something we needed to do."

It wasn't persuasion that made the difference. It was **testing**.
I had a strong opinion—and I didn't demand it be accepted as truth.
He had a strong opinion—and he didn't shut the door when it was challenged.

And because of that, something better was able to emerge.

The most powerful pattern in decision-making isn't certainty—it's testability.

You can hold a strong opinion. You can argue for it, sketch it out, champion it. But if you can't let it be tested, you're not working with a belief—you're working with an identity.

In tech, strong opinions are useful. They give direction. They offer clarity. But the real wisdom is in *how* we hold them. Not like weapons. Not like shields. But like tools—ready to be picked up, put down, or sharpened through experience.

A belief you refuse to test becomes a blind spot.
A belief you *welcome* to be tested becomes a compass.

That's the pattern: **Hold your view with clarity—and release it when reality asks you to.**

Practice: Pause and Release

When you feel strongly about something—pause.

- Ask: *What assumptions am I making?*
- Invite challenge: *Can this be tested, measured, or demonstrated in another way?*
- Stay open: *What would make me change my mind?*

When you're challenged—resist the urge to defend.

- Clarify the intention behind the question.
- Separate your idea from your identity.
- Say, *"Let's try it and see"* more often.

Strong opinions can light the path. But only if you're willing to let the path change beneath your feet.

The first bug is not in the code. It's in the mind that refuses to be wrong. That won't say "I don't know." That confuses experience with truth.

To write great code is to test everything—including your own thinking.
To grow as a developer is to welcome being wrong—not as failure, but as freedom.

Attachment to belief is the first bug.

14

Leadership is Naming the Problem No One Wants to Say

Every team has things it avoids saying. That the deadlines aren't real. That the senior dev's code is full of hidden landmines. That leadership doesn't actually understand the product. That morale is down and people are quietly burning out. These things don't go unsaid because they're unknown — they go unsaid because no one wants to be the first to name them.

We stay silent because we're afraid. Afraid of conflict. Afraid of blame. Afraid of being labeled "negative" or "not a team player." So we hold it in. We keep the peace. We nod in meetings and try to do our jobs in spite of the thing no one's talking about.

But silence doesn't protect us. It gives the problem room to grow. And eventually, it spreads—not just into the system, but into the culture. People stop trusting each other. Bugs go unfixed. Trust erodes. The whole system becomes fragile.

The silent bug is always the most dangerous. Not because no

one sees it—but because everyone sees it, and no one says anything. That's where leadership matters most. Not in solving everything—but in pointing at the thing no one wants to look at and saying, "This isn't working."

Because that's when healing starts. That's where clarity begins.

One of the most consistent patterns in my career is this: I'm the one who asks the questions nobody else seems to want to ask.

Sometimes I'll preface it with, "This might be a stupid question..."—not because I think it's stupid, but because I've learned that the questions everyone's silently stepping around are usually the most important ones. Asking them has, at times, made me trusted. Other times, it's made me unpopular. But it's always been clarifying.

One of the clearest examples of this came during a contract with a client who had a well-established SaaS product—and essentially a one-man IT department. One developer, wearing all the hats, keeping the whole thing afloat. I was brought in to work on a major new UI revamp built off the existing product. The client wanted innovation, polish, and speed. What they didn't have was process, infrastructure, or enough hands on deck.

I worked closely with the developer—making it a two-man team—and started to see the bigger picture. The client leadership had no idea what kind of manpower this new system would actually require. To be fair, the vision wasn't even fully formed yet. But I saw what was coming. And I didn't stay quiet.

As the scope grew, I didn't just nod and go along—I spoke up. I explained why we needed an agile process. I laid out the gap between capacity and expectations. I showed how we could scale. And I brought in people to help fill those gaps.

Within nine months, we went from two people to five.

And that client? Still my client today. The work has evolved. The context has changed. But the foundation—trust, honesty, candor—is what made the relationship last.

Because sometimes leadership isn't a title. It's simply saying the thing everyone else is dancing around, and doing it with enough clarity and care that people can finally move forward.

The pattern is simple: **Say the thing that needs to be said.**

Not with bravado. Not to be provocative.

But to create clarity where there is confusion—and to release tension that's quietly holding everyone hostage.

In every system—technical, organizational, or human—there are bugs that go unspoken. These silent bugs are dangerous. They don't show up in logs or metrics. But you can feel them in hallway conversations, in awkward silences, in the moments where everyone knows *something's off*, but no one wants to be the first to name it.

Leadership isn't just about solving those problems. It's about surfacing them.

Naming them. Holding space for them. So the team, the system, the culture—can begin to heal and move.

It doesn't have to be loud. It just has to be real.

Practice: *Speaking Up Gently*

When something feels off, name it gently.

- Use language like: *"Can we pause here? I think there's something we're not saying."*
- Frame concerns as observations, not accusations.
- Ask if others are sensing it too—invite the room to open up.

When the group avoids something, be the first to speak.

- If no one's asking the hard question, consider: *"What's the question we're not asking here?"*
- Offer your concern calmly and without attachment.
- Normalize saying things like: *"This might be uncomfortable, but it matters."*

If you can't say it publicly, say it privately. But still say it.

Leadership isn't just the courage to act.

It's the clarity to speak—especially when it's easier to stay quiet.

The silent bug is the one that gets you.

Not because it was invisible, but because no one wanted to be the first to point at it. Everyone saw it. Everyone felt it. But silence made it untouchable. Leadership breaks that pattern.

It names the bug.
It surfaces the tension.
Not to assign blame—but to prevent collapse.

The silent bug crashes the system.
Leadership is naming it before it does.

15

Mentorship is Debugging the Mind, Not Just the Code

"For me, success is not about the wins and losses. It's about helping these young fellas be the best versions of themselves on and off the field."
— *Ted Lasso*

In my experience, most developers don't actually struggle with the nuances of code—at least, not anymore. Languages today are relatively readable, consistent, and even familiar to non-developers in some ways. Syntax isn't the battle it used to be.

You might think that after enough experience, those early struggles would fade entirely. That you'd eventually unlock some perfect, frictionless state where you crank out beautiful code, bug-free and unbothered.

That doesn't happen.

Part of the reason is obvious: the tools are always changing.

New languages, frameworks, platforms—it never stops. So even the most experienced developer is constantly a beginner at something. But that's not the whole story.

When you're early in your career, the hardest part is often just getting the code to work. Later, the harder part becomes *everything else*. Explaining a complicated architectural flaw to a business stakeholder who doesn't understand it. Feeling like you're the only one who sees a problem no one wants to talk about. Questioning whether you're actually as good as people think you are.

The best mentors know: most of the struggle isn't in the code— it's in the mind.

It's in the anxiety. The second-guessing. The fear of being seen as slow, or wrong, or not good enough.

When fear takes over, your nervous system goes into fight, flight, or freeze. No amount of syntax knowledge fixes that. A good mentor doesn't just offer solutions—they offer calm. They help you notice the panic. They help you find your footing.

Because before you can fix the bug, you have to calm the system running it.

Have you ever tried fixing a problem in the middle of panic?

I have. More times than I can count.

And even when I've "fixed" it, the results weren't great.

There's a reason first responders are trained not just in protocol, but in managing their own nervous systems under pressure. You can't solve well when your brain is on fire.

My mother-in-law is a Nurse Practitioner—retired Army medical, years of experience in emergencies. She was driving with my oldest daughter when my daughter had a seizure in the car. Instead of immediately calling 911, she called my wife, panicked. She wasn't thinking clearly. The medical training was still in there, but in that moment, it was buried under emotion. I picked up the phone, dialed 911, calmed her down enough to get a location, and got an ambulance on the way.

Even the most experienced people can short-circuit when the panic hits close to home.

I've always kind of thrived in crisis mode. I'll admit that. I've built some of my career on being the one who could "step in" during a mess. But therapy has taught me there's a cost to that—emotionally and mentally—and sometimes it meant I was chasing a sense of control, not clarity. I've had just as many moments where I failed under pressure, even if no one noticed but me.

I remember one developer I worked with—Tom.

Soft-spoken. Smart. Absolutely capable.

But he couldn't function under our boss. The pressure, the micromanagement, the constant tension—it crushed him. He once told me, "I feel like he's always pressing down on me." I tried to empathize, even offered advice, but in truth—I didn't really see the heart of it.

Back then, I still thought I could "fix" the situation by influencing our boss, by architecting my way around the dysfunction. I didn't understand that mentorship isn't about controlling the environment—it's about helping someone *face it*. Helping them understand what they *can* and *can't* change. I didn't help Tom name the truth of his situation, or support him in figuring out his options. He figured it out on his own. One day he left for lunch—and never came back. He emailed that his keys were in his desk.

Looking back, I see it clearly:

His problem wasn't code.
It was panic, pressure, and powerlessness.

And I wasn't the mentor I needed to be—not because I didn't care, but because I hadn't yet learned how to hold space for someone else's storm.

The pattern is this: **Mentorship is presence first, problem-solving second.**

When someone is stuck, overwhelmed, or spiraling, you're not debugging their code—you're debugging their nervous system. And the real root cause is rarely just "they don't understand the syntax." It's usually stress. Imposter syndrome. Feeling like they're behind. Feeling like they don't belong.

You can't refactor anything until the system is stable. That's true for people too.

The best mentors don't just offer advice. They *observe the state*.
They don't just ask "What's the bug?"—they ask, "How are you holding up?"
They build trust before they offer feedback.
They help you slow down, unclench, and see the problem clearly.

Because once the panic subsides, most developers can find their way.

Practice: Calming the Mind

- **Start with the person, not the code.**
  Ask "How are you feeling about this?" before "What's going wrong here?"

- **Watch for signs of panic.**
  If their sentences are rushed, if they keep jumping between files, if they say "I have no idea what I'm doing"—they're in a spiral. Pause. Breathe. Slow it down.

- **Normalize struggle.**
  Say things like "Yeah, this part always trips people up." Or "I remember getting stuck in the exact same place." Let them know they're not broken.

- **Don't solve it for them. Create space for them to see it.**
  Use questions like: "What's the part that feels confusing?"

"What have you tried?"
"What's one small thing we can clarify right now?"

The best mentors don't rush in to fix—they slow things down to *see*.
Calm is the precondition for clarity.
And clarity is where real learning begins.

When a developer is stuck, it's rarely because they lack intelligence. More often, it's because they're overwhelmed. Their mind is racing, their thoughts are scrambled, and they're trying to debug in the middle of an emotional storm.

Mentorship, at its core, is about showing up with steady hands when someone else feels like they're falling apart. It's not about having all the answers—it's about creating enough calm for the answers to emerge.

The calm voice that says, "You're okay. We'll walk through it."
The gentle pause that helps them breathe.
The shift from performance to presence.

Before logic comes breath.
Before clarity comes calm.
To fix the bug, first calm the panic. Only then does the code start to speak again.

IV

The Self in the System

In code and in life, we confuse what we do with who we are. Ego clings, identity warps, and change rattles us. These chapters explore letting go of illusions about permanence, practicing humility, and finding freedom in recognizing that systems, roles, and even we ourselves are always in flux.

16

Your Career is Not Your Codebase

It's dangerously easy to confuse what you *do* with who you *are*. Especially in tech. We spend hours writing code, debugging problems, pushing commits—and eventually, we start to believe our value is measured in diff stats and story points. That's when every bug feels personal. Every review feels like judgment. But the truth is: you are not your pull request. And forgetting that is a bug all its own.

And all of that doing? It gets rewarded. Reinforced.
"You learn by doing."
"You solved the problem no one else could."
"You've earned a promotion."

We get paid more. We build a life around that paycheck. Around that *doing*.

Before long, everything becomes interdependent. Your output becomes your identity. Your career becomes your codebase.

So it's no surprise that bugs start to feel like enemies. That we start chasing them with a kind of religious zeal. Some of us go full Ahab—turning a particularly tricky issue into our white whale. And when someone questions our solution or doesn't understand our fix, it feels like they're questioning *us*.

But that story didn't end well for Ahab.

He wrapped his entire identity around catching that whale—and it sank him.

We need to remember: we are not our pull requests. You can't sum up the life of a human in a list of commits or a velocity chart. We *know* this. And still, we forget.

That forgetting—that deep, human tendency to wrap our worth around what we produce—is perhaps the most foundational "bug" of them all.

I'm a *Doctor Who* fan. Not a superfan, but I've enjoyed all of Nu-Who—especially Eccleston, Tennant, and Smith. There's a scene from the 11th Doctor, Matt Smith, that's burned into my memory. He's in the TARDIS, hacking together some absurd contraption inside the console. Amy and Rory are off somewhere else. The Doctor drops down, hanging upside down, and says:

"I am being extremely clever up here and there's no one to stand around looking impressed. What's the point in having you all?"

At the time that episode aired, I *felt* that. I identified with it completely. I thought I was terribly clever, and I wanted everyone to see it. I was writing good code—there was no doubt about that—but code wasn't just what I did. It was *who I was*. That identity was so tightly woven into my sense of self that everything else in my life started to bend and buckle under the weight of it.

I was in early, stayed late. Every idea I had had to be good. Every disagreement felt like a challenge to *me*, not to the work. It would take me another decade—and several massive failures—to start unlearning that.

In that decade, I lived a lot. I created and lost two businesses. Went through two separations and nearly lost my marriage. Almost failed out of college a second time. Lived through constant anxiety—whether about work, money, or one of my four kids. Each new chapter became the next thing I wrapped my identity around: husband, founder, father, student. Every role became the whole story.

One of those businesses, I built over four years. It grew into a contracting firm with over a dozen people—ten of them billing. I was the CEO, and it had my name on it. I was all in. But I made mistakes. Trusted the wrong people. And I was pushed out in a storm of stress, arguments, and tension.

The month that followed was one of the hardest of my life. I had to pick up pieces. I had to let go of a lot more.

Thankfully, a client offered me work. I found my footing. And slowly, I started asking a better question:

75

"Who am I if I'm not the job? If I'm not the title? If I'm not the code?"

That question hasn't left me.
I don't think it ever will.
And that's probably a good thing.

So what made the difference?

After the collapse of that identity—CEO, builder, fixer—I was already in therapy. I'd been working on myself for a while. Everyone can benefit from therapy, but I'm not the easiest client. I'm stubborn. I'm an engineer. I thought I could out-think my own brain. Hack my emotional system. Optimize my mental health like I'd optimize code.

Turns out, that doesn't work.

What helped was someone else asking *me* the kinds of questions I was used to asking other people. And slowly, I began to notice something profound: I could *observe* my feelings instead of *being* them. I could experience an emotion without letting it run the show. I could *see* my thoughts without clinging to them. I could care deeply about the work—without becoming the work.

This is the shift.

One of the most important moves you can make as a developer is to stop *identifying* with your output and start *observing* it.

You are not your bug report.

You are not your code review.
You're not the file.
You're the author.

And authors?
They revise. They grow.
They know when to let go.

Practice: Holding Yourself Lightly

- **Name, Pause, Release**

  When feedback stings or a bug hits harder than it should, pause. Name the feeling. "I feel embarrassed." "I feel defensive." Just naming it creates space. Then ask yourself: *What part of me is feeling threatened?* You'll often find it's not the code—it's your identity. The moment you see that, you can start to let go.

- **Detach Without Disconnecting**

  Your code is not a confession—it's a conversation. Treat your pull requests like drafts, not declarations. When you review your own code, do it like you would for a teammate: with clarity and care. When something goes wrong, replace *Why did I mess this up?* with *What is this trying to teach me?*

· **Build Your Identity Stack**

List the roles you hold beyond "developer." Parent. Partner. Friend. Teacher. Creator. Spend time with those identities— nurture them. When one role takes a hit, the others help you stay grounded. This is how you build resilience that isn't brittle.

No one's going to remember the exact code you wrote.
Not five years from now. Maybe not even five months.
But they'll remember *how* you showed up.
They'll remember if you listened. If you were kind. If you shared.
They'll remember if you made the work better—*and* made the room better.

The work matters. But the person behind the work?
That's what leaves the real legacy.

17

Ego Writes Fragile Code

"Your scientists were so preoccupied with whether they could, they didn't stop to think if they should."
— *Dr. Ian Malcolm, Jurassic Park*

If you're anything like me, you've probably been reading through a section of code, hit a confusing block, and thought, *"Who wrote this?!"* Then you pull up git blame, and realize it was you, six months ago. That's always a fun moment. You suddenly see that Past You was very clever, but not especially kind.

It's a perfect example of ego turning into technical debt. Quiet at first, then suddenly expensive. That code was over-defended, under-explained, and more about proving something than solving something. Ego wants control. But code doesn't need to be controlled—it needs to be understood.

And here's the thing: we don't run git blame on great code. We don't care who wrote the piece that just works, that flows, that feels obvious in the best way. When you disappear into the work—not because you're erasing yourself, but because you're clear and grounded—the code becomes stronger. Cleaner. Easier to live with. When you stop trying to impress, you actually start to express.

One of the last major projects I took on at a previous job was to integrate three distinct systems—each with its own database and UI—into something that felt like a single, decentralized platform. These systems had related functionality but were completely siloed. Today, we'd lean on established tools and patterns for this. But at the time, many of those didn't exist, and I was working in a .NET world where WCF was the go-to for services.

So, I started architecting. I wanted two-way communication. I wanted robustness. Retries. Extensibility. Every bell and whistle I could think of. I laid out my design and got buy-in—not because everyone understood it, but because they trusted me to get it done. I called it the "integration services," built the first implementation, wired it into one of the three products, and then helped get it hooked into the others. It worked. Technically.

But I defended that design like it was sacred. Anytime someone questioned it, I pushed back hard. And in the end, no one else touched it—because no one else understood it. After I left, a friend who stayed on told me they eventually ripped it out and replaced it with simple direct calls between the systems.

Looking back, I realized I had been trying to build an event bus. Something like a primitive Kafka or RabbitMQ, before those were common tools. But I wasn't clear about that even to myself. I wasn't trying to solve a real, shared problem. I was trying to architect something impressive. And in the process, I wrote code that was clever, but fragile. Maybe it's better that it didn't survive.

There's a place for complexity. Any senior developer knows that not all problems can be solved with a simple if statement and a clean interface. But complexity should serve clarity, not vanity. The question isn't whether the solution is elegant or impressive. The question is whether the next person can understand it.

If you're introducing a framework, a pattern, or a new abstraction, stop and ask: Does this make the system easier to understand? Or just harder to question? There's a difference between building something powerful and building something nobody else can challenge.

Real strength isn't found in sophistication that demands obedience. It's found in simplicity that invites understanding.

Practice: Disappearing

- Refactor your code until it feels like anyone could have written it.
- Favor descriptive, human-centered names over poetic cleverness.
- Treat code reviews as a dialogue, not a defense.
- Let the next developer feel like they belong here, too.

Your code is not your monument. It is not your legacy. It is a tool—built to be used, changed, and eventually replaced. Ego turns that into loss. But humility sees it for what it is: a contribution made in a moment, part of a larger whole.

Letting go doesn't mean vanishing. It means releasing the need for credit. It means trusting that the work, if done with care, will outlive your name. To let go is not to disappear. It's to integrate. And that's where real strength begins.

18

Like All Things, This Too Changes

Nothing in software—or life—stays the same. Codebases evolve. Tools change. Teams reshuffle. Titles come and go. And yet, most of us cling to something, whether it's an identity, a role, or even the elegant code we hope will outlast us. When someone questions whether we've considered that our title might vanish or our proudest work might be sunsetted, our reaction often says more than our answer.

We're taught that everything changes. But accepting that change is a different matter. Knowing something isn't the same as being at peace with it. Losing a job, watching a project we poured ourselves into get shelved—these things still hurt. And often, we resist. We "should" ourselves into suffering: "*It shouldn't be this way. It must work out.*" We argue with reality, and reality doesn't flinch.

There are those who seem able to radically accept all the changes life throws their way. This isn't resignation. It's not giving up or pretending not to care. It's the steady practice of facing change without flinching. Not avoiding it. Not resenting it, but just seeing it clearly. When we stop fixating on what's slipping away, we begin to notice what's still here—and what might be possible next.

I've shared earlier how I lost the business I had built—but I haven't talked much about what that *felt* like. When it happened, I went through every stage of grief. First came denial: *This can't be happening.* Then anger—at the people who made those choices, and at myself for trusting them with that power. I bargained, tried to make deals over equipment. I spiraled into sadness, some days not wanting to get out of bed. And while I told myself I had "accepted" it, it took a long time to reach anything close to true acceptance.

So much of my identity was tied up in being the founder, the CEO, the one who others looked to for mentorship and leadership. When all that vanished—when even the people I'd supported for years stopped talking to me—I felt hollow. And worse, I felt *wrong* for being angry or sad. Like I wasn't allowed to feel those things. But eventually, I got more honest with myself. I found work that kept me afloat. I hired legal help. I handed over what was asked of me and focused in on what came next.

And that's when something shifted. I had time again. I had space. I realized I was no longer tethered to that old thing— or the weight it carried. I started to rebuild. I clarified what I truly valued. And slowly, I saw the change not as a loss, but as a clearing. An unexpected beginning, disguised as an end.

Change is not an edge case, it's a system constraint. We treat latency, memory, and architecture as fundamental to good design, but too often treat change like an afterthought. In truth, nothing in software is permanent. Not your favorite framework. Not your current title. Not even the company you work for. If you build with the assumption that things will stay as they are, you're building in fragility. When you acknowledge impermanence as the default, not the exception, you begin to design systems—and careers—that adapt instead of break.

Practice: Accepting and Designing for Change

- Assume every title, tool, and team will change—because they will.
- Build systems and habits with the next person in mind.
- Document decisions clearly, especially the *why* behind them.
- Practice refactoring not just your code, but your thinking.
- Expect to be replaced, and treat that as a success, not a failure.

Everything you build will change. So will your team, your role, your priorities—and yes, even you. This isn't a reason for despair. It's not a failure of stability. It's a feature of life. The sooner you accept that change is the rule, not the exception, the more skillfully you can respond to it.

Impermanence gives you permission to stop clinging—to code, to status, to the comfort of the familiar. When you loosen your grip, you become more adaptable, more thoughtful, and more generous in your work. You start writing code for others, not just for yourself. You start mentoring not to control, but to elevate. You make better decisions—not because you're certain, but because you're present.

When you recognize change as inevitable, you stop resisting it. You start flowing with it. And in doing so, you become a better coder, a better teammate, and maybe even a better human.

19

Let Go or Be Dragged

"The more you tighten your grip, Tarkin, the more star systems will
slip through your fingers."
— *Princess Leia, Star Wars*

You've felt it before: the project going sideways, the tech debt
piling up, the leadership making demands that don't align with
the reality on the ground. In those moments, it's tempting
to hold tighter—to control the process, the people, even the
perception of what's happening. But control isn't clarity. It's a
fear response.

In tech, white-knuckling your way through complexity usually
leads to brittle systems and burned-out teams. The more tightly
we grip to the original plan, the more we fight change instead of
flowing with it. Whether it's an architectural decision, a team
dynamic, or a personal expectation, we must learn when to hold
on with intention and when to let go with grace.

Letting go is not the same as giving up. It's a move from fear to trust. And trust, in ourselves and in the system around us, is what makes space for real stability.

I've led teams through crunches—and sometimes, one crunch bleeds right into the next. In one particular stretch, the pressure never seemed to let up. Sprint after sprint, we were shipping constantly, reacting constantly, and questioning whether our Agile process was working at all. When you're living in that cycle long enough, it stops feeling agile and starts feeling like a treadmill.

I was at the top. The buck stopped with me. And I didn't just feel responsible for the outcomes—we were also managing a client relationship, and I took it upon myself to manage their emotions, too. I believed every problem had a solution, and so I kept looking for one. More meetings. More structure. More oversight on pull requests. More leadership from me. But it wasn't clarity I was creating—it was control. And I was burning out.

The problem was: I didn't know it. No one around me was telling me either, because their livelihoods depended on me continuing. It wasn't the kind of burnout you fix with a long weekend. The minute I came back from any break, the problems would still be there—along with the pressure to perform, to lead, to hold everything together. What I needed was a paradigm shift. One that let go of the illusion of control I thought I needed to maintain.

I wouldn't learn that lesson until years later, when I had to rebuild everything. Looking back, I can see it clearly: if I had stepped back from control, trusted the team more, and made the hard but necessary cuts, I might have lost some friendships—but I wouldn't have lost the company. I gripped too tightly. And it all slipped through my fingers.

Control feels safe—especially for engineers and leaders. But in truth, it's often a mask for fear. The tighter we cling, the more we convince ourselves that control will bring certainty, significance, or connection. And in that moment, it *feels* like it's working. But what we're really doing is building a fragile structure around unmet needs.

If you don't know which of your core needs you're trying to protect—certainty, variety, significance, love and connection, growth, or contribution—then your need for control will quietly drive decisions that put those very needs at risk. When we grip too tightly, we lose adaptability. Codebases that are over-engineered become brittle. Teams that are micromanaged lose trust. Leaders who try to hold everything alone end up isolated.

Control doesn't guarantee safety. It often guarantees stagnation. The alternative is not chaos, it's awareness, intention, and a willingness to trust.

Practice: A Checklist for Letting Go

- **Notice the grip** – are you tightening your hold out of fear, frustration, or fatigue? Pause before reacting.
- **Name the need** – ask: *What am I trying to protect?* Identify which core human need—certainty, significance, love, growth, variety, or contribution—is pulling the strings.

- **Share the burden** – delegate not just tasks, but trust. Let others step in without needing to control the outcome.
- **Shrink the scope** – focus on what's truly in your circle of control, and let go of the rest.
- **Recommit with clarity** – letting go isn't giving up. It's choosing to move forward with presence, not panic.

The hardest part of letting go is not the act itself—it's untangling the meaning we've attached to holding on. We fear that if we release control, we've somehow failed. That we've given up. That we weren't strong enough. But what if the real strength lies in trust? In loosening our grip on the illusion that we're the only thing holding it all together?

The truth is, white-knuckling through change doesn't preserve what we care about—it corrodes it. It isolates us from our teams. It burdens our minds. And slowly, it hardens the joy right out of the work. Letting go isn't apathy or absence. It's a reorientation. It's choosing to stay fully present in what's real, instead of clinging to what we hoped would be.

So when the pressure builds, and you feel yourself tightening, ask gently: what story am I trying to protect? And is that story still serving me—or dragging me?

20

The Job is Temporary. The Impact Might Not Be.

My dad stayed with the same company for over 30 years. He navigated layoffs, made himself indispensable, and retired with the kind of loyalty badge that used to mean something. My path? A bit different. I've built things, walked away from them, lost them, and started again.

Still, no matter where I've been, one thing stays with me: the legacy I leave behind. I love hearing that a process I set up is still saving people time. I quietly flinch when I hear that my code got scrapped or rewritten. Not out of ego—but because I care. I care about what lasts after I'm gone.

Jobs are temporary. Projects evolve. Code gets deleted. But people remember the patterns you set, the tone you carried, and how you made their work feel. That's your impact. You won't be here forever. The next coder will.

My dad spent over three decades with the same employer,

and loyalty meant staying. For my generation, loyalty means showing up, doing the work, and knowing when it's time to move forward.

Each time I've moved on, I've made a point to keep in touch. Not just to stay connected, but because I genuinely care about what happens after I leave. One of my favorite things is hearing that a pattern I helped put in place is still working. A tool I introduced still saves someone time. A bit of guidance I offered helped someone navigate a hard moment. On the flip side, I've felt the sting when something I poured time into was tossed out or reworked without context. That craving for legacy? It's real. So is the aversion to seeing your work disappear. But both of those feelings point to something deeper.

It's not about the permanence of code. It's about the impression you leave on people. Code gets rewritten. Tools get replaced. But people remember how you showed up—whether you helped or hindered, whether you made their lives easier or harder. That's the kind of legacy we carry forward, whether we know it or not.

I've actually worked at the same company as my father not once, but twice—first as a teenager during a summer internship, and again years later as an adult. That company and that time shaped me in ways I didn't fully grasp until much later. One of the most valuable things I observed during those years was how my dad moved through the workplace. He had a way of "rocking the boat" without capsizing it. He could say the honest thing—the thing no one else wanted to say—but he knew how to say it in a way that made people trust him more, not less.

When I was younger, I tried to emulate that, but I hadn't quite picked up on the subtlety. I rocked the boat too hard, too fast. That didn't always serve me well, but it taught me something important: your presence makes ripples. And those ripples shape the culture more than most policies ever will.

In every company, the real legacy isn't the stack you leave behind. It's the norms you reinforce, the truths you're willing to name, and the tone you help set. Culture remembers. And if we're intentional, we can choose what kind of ripple we leave behind.

Takeaway: The Culture You Leave Behind

- **Mentor someone who's newer than you.** Even just pairing once or twice can shape their perspective for years.
- **Model calm during chaos.** How you react under pressure teaches others what's "normal."
- **Normalize speaking up with care.** It doesn't have to be loud—it just has to be honest.
- **Clean up behind yourself.** Write the docs, refactor the function, remove the sharp edge. Someone will thank you later.

You won't be remembered for your pull requests. But you might be remembered for how you helped a teammate through a hard bug, how you advocated for someone's idea in a meeting, or how you led with kindness when pressure was high. The code fades. The culture remains. And it's your choice which parts of yourself leave lasting echoes.

V

Practices for the Mindful Developer

The work isn't just what you ship—it's how you show up. These chapters share habits that foster awareness, clarity, and care in your craft. By practicing intentionality in your daily actions, you build systems—and a self—that can thrive without burning out.

21

Start with Stillness (Again)

"Slow is smooth, and smooth is fast."
— *US Navy SEAL proverb*

Most software engineers don't write bad code because they're bad developers. They write bad code because they're in a hurry. Because someone's waiting. Because there's pressure. Because their nervous system is still vibrating from the last meeting.

In a world obsessed with speed, stillness feels like rebellion. But in reality, it's a return to sanity. It's not inactivity—it's intention. When we start from stillness, we invite clarity into the room. We pause long enough to see what's actually needed—not just what's loudest.

The practice of beginning in stillness echoes foundational teachings in mindfulness and Buddhism. When we sit and breathe—even briefly—we loosen the grip of reactivity. We step out of the loop of conditioned responses and into a moment of conscious engagement. Like a developer reading the diff before typing a single line, we become aware of the ground we're standing on before we build upon it.

Stillness isn't a one-time fix. It's a muscle, a practice. One that sharpens with repetition and reshapes how we show up to our work, our teams, and ourselves.

There was a stretch in my career when I lived in constant motion. Meetings, Slack pings, code reviews, production emergencies—one bleeding into the next. I thought moving fast meant I cared, that speed was the best way to prove value. But over time, I saw my thinking deteriorate. I'd react to messages with a sharp tone I regretted later. I'd push code that felt rushed, brittle, sloppy. Even when I knew better, I couldn't break the cycle.

Almost out of desperation, I tried something small: forcing myself to take just three minutes of stillness before starting any significant task. No music, no scrolling, no problem-solving—just breathing. Sometimes I'd stare out a window. Sometimes I'd walk to the kitchen and back. Sometimes I'd close my eyes at my desk. Slowly, I noticed a shift. I caught bad assumptions before they hardened into bad decisions. I spoke more clearly. I wrote better code—not slower, but better.

Then I tried something even more specific: meditating for five minutes before opening my IDE each morning. The idea came after reading about how your mental state at the *start* of a task shapes everything that follows. So I figured, sit, breathe, then code.

The first few times, I was terrified someone would walk by and think I'd fallen asleep sitting up. So I printed a tiny sign that read "5-Minute Mindfulness, not dead" and taped it to the back of my chair.

It was silly, but it worked. I found myself less fused to my code, more willing to hear feedback, more patient when things broke, and less judgmental of myself when a solution took longer than expected. That silly five-minute pause helped me reclaim presence—and made every part of my work better.

Our nervous systems are wired for speed. When we sense pressure, uncertainty, or a hint of threat—whether it's a tense meeting or a looming deadline—the sympathetic nervous system kicks in. Our bodies prepare for fight, flight, or freeze. Our breath becomes shallow. Our field of vision narrows. Our thinking grows rigid and reactive. We become primed to *do something*, even if it's the wrong thing entirely.

That's why starting in stillness is so powerful: it interrupts this automatic cascade. A deliberate pause—a deep breath, a few moments of quiet—activates the parasympathetic nervous system, the branch responsible for calming us down. This shift widens our awareness, loosens mental rigidity, and restores access to creativity and reason.

The habit of pausing doesn't just slow you down; it helps you break the loop of reactivity. It gives you a small but powerful gap where you can choose your response instead of being hijacked by old patterns. Stillness is the entry point to presence—and presence is where better decisions, clearer communication, and wiser code can begin.

Practice: Daily Stillness Habits

The One-Minute Breath

- Before opening your IDE, close your eyes and take ten slow breaths.
- Count each inhale and exhale to anchor your mind.
- Let your shoulders drop and your jaw unclench.
- Begin your work from this calm, intentional space.

The Transition Ritual

- Between meetings or major tasks, take 60 seconds with no screens.
- Stand up, stretch, or look out a window.
- Silently label your emotional state—e.g., "frustrated," "excited," "nervous."
- Breathe. Then start the next thing with presence.

Before you write a single line, remember: the quality of your work starts with the quality of your attention. The mind you bring to the keyboard shapes the clarity, stability, and purpose of what you build. When you begin with stillness, you set the tone for everything that follows.

Stillness isn't passive. It's a powerful act of presence. It's the moment where you choose to observe instead of react, to listen instead of rush. It's how you move from frantic guessing to intentional understanding.

The quieter you become, the more you hear—not just in the code, but in the subtle signals around you. The overlooked detail in the requirements. The unspoken tension in the team. The truth of your own state of mind.

In stillness, you lay the foundation of awareness beneath your work. And in that awareness, you find the clarity to build not just better software, but a better way of being.

22

Walk the Code Once Before You Fix It

You wouldn't re-wire an entire house just because you found a switch that doesn't seem to control anything. And yet, developers make this exact mistake in their code all the time, ripping and replacing large sections because something looks confusing or broken at first glance. It's hard to find a reason for this impulse that doesn't come down to arrogance, ego, or impatience. And more often than not, that single "small" rewrite spirals into a massive refactor.

Taking the time to read through the code—especially when the patterns are unfamiliar—can feel daunting or like a waste of time. But it's exactly what saves us from making bad assumptions. You can't fix what you don't understand. Instead of arrogantly thinking, *"Whatever I write will be a thousand times better than this,"* put that idea down and read the code first.

Interestingly, there's one area where today's AI coding assistants struggle: troubleshooting and bug fixing. Why? Because they're quick to propose sweeping refactors rather than carefully tracing through existing logic to make a precise correction. When it comes to fixing complex systems, the scalpel will always do less damage than the hammer.

When I became a lead developer for the first time (and trust me, it wasn't glamorous; I was the only person I was leading), I was still early in my career. The system I was working on had a permissions model built in-house by the previous lead. I knew the permissions tables existed, and everything seemed to work fine. That is, until I added a new primary area to the application and realized no one could see it but me.

I'd added a record for the new feature into the permissions table, copying values from another record. One of the columns held a strange-looking string I didn't understand. My first instinct was to tear out the whole permissions setup and rebuild it in a simpler, more modern way. But my colleague and mentor, Bob, advised me to slow down. He suggested we walk the code together first.

For the next hour, we traced how permissions were set, checked, and applied. Along the way, we ran into something I'd never seen before: **bitmasking,** a way of storing many boolean (yes/no) states compactly in a single integer by representing each as a different bit. For example, with bitmasking, a permission integer of five (binary 0101) could mean permissions one and three are enabled while others are not. It's a clever way to encode multiple on/off flags in one place.

On top of that, I learned that these bitmask values were stored as encrypted strings in the database to prevent anyone from directly manipulating permissions in client copies of the database, a layer of security I hadn't considered but could appreciate.

Had I impulsively rewritten the permissions system, I would have created a mountain of extra work for myself and possibly broken things I didn't yet understand. By taking the time to fully grasp the existing code, I was able not only to fix the issue at hand but also to extend permissions with finer control over the new feature. Bob's advice taught me an enduring lesson: that patience and careful study often move you faster in the long run than arrogance and haste ever could.

The instinct to rewrite is natural—especially when code looks confusing or outdated. There's a certain rush to ripping something out and building it "right" from scratch. But that rush often masks impatience or ego, and the fastest way to cause regressions is to change what you don't fully understand.

Reading the existing code first, even when it feels slow, prevents careless mistakes. It gives you the context to see why something was done the way it was, what edge cases it handles, and what dependencies it touches. You start to see the system as a whole, not just as disconnected pieces. What looked like a mess might actually reveal thoughtful decisions layered over time.

Understanding before you act isn't wasted effort—it's the foundation of real confidence. It allows you to make changes with precision and respect for what already works. And it turns fixing a problem from an act of reckless force into an act of mindful craftsmanship.

Practice: Three Ways to Walk the Code

The Two-Pass Rule

- Before making any changes, read the code twice: once for a surface understanding, once for details.
- Write a short summary of what the code is doing and why you think it was written that way.
- Only then decide whether a change is truly needed—or if a smaller fix will suffice.

The Debugger's Walk

- Step through the code in a debugger, line by line, watching how values flow.
- Make notes about assumptions you had going in—and what the code actually does.
- If you find surprises, adjust your plan before touching anything.

Pair-Reading Practice

- Invite a teammate to read the code together before changing it.
- Explain your understanding out loud, and encourage questions.
- This not only catches blind spots but also spreads knowledge across the team.

Reading is an act of respect—for the code, for its history, and for the people who will come after you. When you start by truly understanding, you build with clarity instead of ego. Every line you read carefully today saves confusion for someone tomorrow—including you.

23

Make Commit Messages a Journal of Intent

"Words are, in my not-so-humble opinion, our most inexhaustible source of magic."
— Albus Dumbledore, *Harry Potter and the Deathly Hallows*

The most recurring theme every software developer encounters is a lack of documentation. Over time, you start to realize there may never be a point where the documentation feels "enough." But that doesn't mean we shouldn't keep trying to close the gap.

We have plenty of ways to document our code: Wikis, code comments, architecture diagrams. And let's be honest—if you use git or any source control system (and if you don't, please start), you'll eventually be the person running git blame to figure out who made these changes and why.

That brings us to a place where most developers—including myself—fall short: commit messages. Commit messages are the journal entries of your codebase, but they're often written like cryptic tweets. "Fix thing," "oops," or "stuff works now" don't help anyone. If we put a bit more effort into documenting our changes in these messages, our intent will come across much more quickly to future readers of our code.

Because the difference between a mess and a legacy isn't just the code; it's how well you explain your thinking. Leave a breadcrumb trail your future self—and everyone else—can actually follow.

I once worked with a developer whose commit messages read like concise, clear stories. Each message included what changed, why it changed, and often even context about what had been tried before. Reading their commit history felt like a guided tour of the codebase—each step illuminated, every decision documented. It was the first time I realized that good commit messages turn a chaotic project into a teachable artifact. A codebase with well-written commits becomes an archaeological record you can actually learn from, not just guess at.

That experience taught me that good commit messages don't just happen by accident. They come from developers who care about the story their code tells. It reminded me of the example set by Linus Torvalds himself—one of the most respected figures in software. His own commits show a consistent structure: a single-line imperative header summarizing the change, followed by a clear explanation of the reasoning behind it. Torvalds emphasizes that commit messages should explain *why* a change was made, not just *what* was done, so that both reviewers and future maintainers can understand the thinking behind the solution.

In Buddhist philosophy, right speech comes from right intention: it aims to be truthful, clear, and helpful. Commit messages can follow the same principle. They are our speech within the codebase—our words to the future developers, teammates, and even ourselves.

Messages written with clarity, honesty, and context strengthen understanding across the lifespan of a system. They reduce confusion, build trust in the codebase, and make collaboration easier. Meanwhile, vague, defensive, or misleading commit messages act like careless words; they sow confusion, frustrate maintainers, and erode confidence in the work.

When we approach commit messages as right speech, we move beyond documenting actions to documenting intention—turning each message into a small act of stewardship for our shared code.

Practice: Writing Meaningful Commit Messages

The following is an example of a commit message standard directly from Linus Torvalds.

```
Header line: explain the commit in one line (use the
imperative)

Body of commit message is a few lines of text,
explaining things
in more detail, possibly giving some background about
the issue
```

```
being fixed, etc.

The body of the commit message can be several
paragraphs, and
please do proper word-wrap and keep columns shorter
than about
74 characters or so. That way "git log" will show
things
nicely even when it's indented.

Make sure you explain your solution and why you're
doing what you're
doing, as opposed to describing only what you're
doing. Reviewers
and your future self can read the patch, but might
not understand
why a particular solution was implemented.

Reported-by: whoever-reported-it
Signed-off-by: Your Name <youremail@yourhost.com>
```

Remember:

- The header line should be meaningful and stand alone—this is what shows up in tools like git log and should summarize the change in one clear line.
- Use verbs in the imperative, like "Fix bug..." or "Add validation..."
- Focus on explaining the *why* as much as the *what*. Context today is clarity tomorrow.

A commit message is more than a log; it's a window into your thought process. When you write with intention, you turn silent diffs into a conversation—one that can teach, clarify, and build trust across time.

The difference between chaos and clarity isn't just in the code; it's in how we explain it. Commit messages are your chance to transform confusion into connection. Commit not just your changes, but your intentions. The code will change. The understanding you leave will last.

24

Practice Deleting More Than You Add

In software, we often measure our worth by what we build: the new features, the clever optimizations, the impressive architectural layers. But experienced developers know that the true art is in subtraction. The more code you can remove without losing functionality, the clearer the system becomes.

Like a sculptor revealing form by chipping away stone, clarity in code emerges when we let go of what no longer serves. Every unnecessary function, redundant check, or outdated workaround clouds the purpose of a system. Each one is a small distraction for the next person who reads it—including your future self.

Deleting code isn't about being reckless. It's about questioning assumptions, revisiting what's essential, and honoring simplicity over complexity. In a world where software naturally grows more tangled with time, practicing deliberate removal is an act of respect for your work and everyone who touches it.

One of my best clients has a 30-year-old codebase. Of course, not every line of it is that old, but the system has been continuously built and evolved over three decades. The sheer amount of code is daunting. In the first phase of the projects I worked on with them, we didn't even try to touch it. But as the work progressed, it became clear that utilizing parts of the existing codebase would accelerate what we needed to deliver.

My instinct was to pair closely with my counterpart on their team so we could really understand what we were modifying. That process revealed what you'd expect in a codebase that old: a lot of outdated patterns and ways of doing things. As languages evolve, they introduce features that change how we write and design code. So we took a proactive approach—modernizing the areas we needed as we built new features.

This approach let us update and replace large swaths of code in a careful, testable way. We gained the benefits of both abstraction and subtraction: more efficient, more readable code doing the same work, with configuration as the key differentiator. Most of my pull requests ended up with negative line counts (not that that's the ultimate measure of value). But it was the most satisfying work I've done—clearing away the old to make room for the new—and probably the biggest reason I still work with that client to this day.

Code rarely improves with age. Patterns grow stale, workarounds accumulate, and complexity compounds quietly over time. What once seemed like a clever solution can become a brittle liability as requirements evolve and technology advances. Left unchecked, old code becomes a breeding ground for hidden bugs and unnecessary friction for every developer who comes after you.

Regularly pruning outdated or redundant code isn't about erasing progress—it's about honoring the present needs of the system. By clearing away what no longer serves, you make space for cleaner patterns, simpler logic, and easier maintenance. This practice keeps systems healthier, teams happier, and the codebase more understandable.

Deleting code thoughtfully is an act of stewardship. It's how you make sure your work doesn't just add value today but stays resilient and adaptable tomorrow.

Practice: Make Deletion a Habit

The Refactor Walk

- When working in an area of code, look for opportunities to remove dead or duplicated logic.
- Delete unused functions, obsolete feature flags, or leftover experimental code.
- If you're unsure, leave comments during review proposing deletions so the team can discuss.

Codebase Spring Cleaning

- Schedule regular time (quarterly or twice a year) to review and prune legacy parts of the codebase.
- Pair with a teammate to avoid deleting critical but poorly

documented code.
- Document what you remove and why, so others understand and don't reintroduce similar complexity later.

Good code isn't just what you add, it's what you choose to leave out. Deleting unnecessary lines creates space for what really matters. In that space, systems become clearer, minds become calmer, and your work becomes more meaningful.

25

Close the Laptop With Intention

"Life moves pretty fast. If you don't stop and look around once in a while, you could miss it."
— Ferris Bueller

How you end your workday matters. It's easy to let tasks spill into your evening—to leave Slack open, to refresh your inbox one more time, to keep turning a bug or a conversation over in your mind while you're cooking dinner or trying to relax. Without a clear boundary, work never truly ends (and rest never truly begins).

Closing the laptop with intention is a small but powerful ritual. It signals to your mind and body: the day is done. You did what you could today, and tomorrow will bring a new chance. In that intentional pause, you give yourself permission to let go of work thoughts and return fully to your life outside the keyboard.

When we skip this pause, we carry tension forward, blurring the lines between presence and distraction. But by ending each day with clarity (even something as simple as a few deep breaths before shutting the laptop) we remind ourselves that good work includes good rest. The day is complete. You can pick it up tomorrow, but for now, you can just be.

There was a time in my life when I could fairly be called a workaholic (really? You don't say!). I'd get up at 4:30 AM some days, head into the office, stay until after 6 PM, and even once I got home, my mind wasn't there, it was still stuck at work. People around me were impressed with what I could accomplish. I soaked in that validation, chasing it like it could somehow make the time spent worthwhile, or maybe justify the sacrifices I was making.

Maybe, in some ways, it was justified. I built a successful company. I brought in a lot of money. I provided for others. I built systems for clients that are still in use. I mentored developers who continue to stay in touch with me. From the outside, it probably looked like I was doing a lot of winning.

But the truth was, I wasn't happy. I wasn't content. Sure, I had moments of happiness, but I was never at peace with how things were. All that relentless work, and the constant search for validation, was me trying to *force* myself to feel content, except that's not how contentment works. Contentment doesn't come from adding more accomplishments; it comes from being fully present with what is, without needing it to be different.

I struggled with this for a long time. My marriage was affected. My relationship with my kids suffered. Like any addiction, my addiction to work was hurting me and those I loved. I had convinced myself my only worth was in what I could produce— and I built my entire identity around that. Then things started to fall apart. When my home life crumbled, I realized something had to change. I got into therapy and began searching for a new way to live.

It took a long time, but one core realization stood out: I can only find contentment and joy in work if there are meaningful periods where I'm *not* working. How can you feel gratitude for something if you're always immersed in it? How can you miss someone you're constantly around? Transitions matter. Without them we get stuck in the same loop. We can get stuck in work, in distraction, even in leisure. And when we're stuck, we lose presence. We disconnect from ourselves and those around us.

But when we wake up, pause, and intentionally end what we're doing—whether it's the workday, a meeting, or a moment of distraction—we snap back to the present. We return to ourselves.

Parenting will teach you a lot of things, but one of the clearest lessons is how much children struggle with transitions. I never considered it until I found myself trying to get my kids ready to leave the house while they were happily immersed in building Legos. (To be fair, I still struggle to transition out of Legos myself.)

What I wasn't equipped to do when I was younger—something that hurt me again and again—was to manage the intense feelings that come when our little bubble of focus is interrupted. Think about it: you're in your own world, deep in flow, and suddenly something or someone breaks in. It feels like an invasion. There's fear that you'll lose your place or won't get back to what you were doing. Those feelings can trigger anger, resentment, or frustration. But all they really do is deepen our suffering.

Transitions are part of life. They're not interruptions to resist but thresholds to cross with awareness. When we practice ending what we're doing with intention—whether it's work, a conversation, or a moment of play—we ease the shift from one state to another. We reduce resistance, reclaim presence, and find more peace in the spaces between.

Practice: Recognizing and Releasing Stuckness

- **Notice the Stuckness**
  Pay attention to moments when you're deep in an activity but can't seem to let it go, even when it's time. Signs of being stuck include feeling irritated by interruptions, losing track of time, or ignoring signals that you need a break.
- **Name the Feeling**
  When you sense yourself resisting a transition, silently name what you're feeling—e.g., "anxious," "excited," "frustrated." Naming helps create distance between you and the emotion, giving you space to choose how to respond.
- **Set an Intentional End**
  Before moving on, pause for a few breaths. Consciously acknowledge the completion of what you were doing. You

119

might think, *"This is done for now,"* or *"I'll pick this up tomorrow."* Then close your laptop, stand up, or physically change your environment.

· **Reflect on the Pattern**
At the end of your day, briefly reflect: When did you get stuck today? What helped you transition out of it? Recognizing your patterns helps you catch them sooner next time.

The day's tasks, wins, and struggles are complete. Let them be. When you release what's done, you create space to return to yourself, your loved ones, and the simple joy of just being. Let the day end so tomorrow can truly begin.

Appendix: Chapter List with Original Koans

This book borrows the structure of the Zen koan—not as a religious teaching, but as a way to hold a question open in the mind. In traditional Zen practice, a koan is a short, often paradoxical statement or question meant to nudge the student beyond easy answers. The point isn't to "solve" it, but to live with it until it changes you.

For each chapter, I've paired a modern koan—something drawn from the world of software, teams, and tech culture—with a classic or adapted Zen koan that inspired it. You don't need to know anything about Zen to find meaning here. Think of these as two lenses pointed at the same idea: one grounded in code, the other in centuries-old reflection.

Use this section to quickly revisit each chapter's core question and its source of inspiration. You may find that, just like code, these koans reveal new insights each time you return to them.

Part I: The Way of the Coder

Mindset, presence, and the inner life of the developer

Start With Stillness

Modern Koan: "Before you write code, calm the coder."
Original Koan: "When the mind is nowhere, it is everywhere."

Read Code Like It's a Story

Modern Koan: "The code speaks. Are you listening?"
Original Koan: "Listen to the sound of one hand clapping."

Before AI, Review Code. After AI, Review Code.

Modern Koan: "The tools evolve. The attention remains."
Original Koan: "Before enlightenment, chop wood, carry water. After enlightenment, chop wood, carry water."

Clarity is Kindness — Even in Code

Modern Koan: "To write clearly is to care for the reader."
Original Koan: "Do not mistake the finger pointing at the moon for the moon itself."

Unattached to the Outcome. Focused on the Process.

Modern Koan: "The build may fail. The practice continues."
Original Koan: "Let go or be dragged."

Part II: The Tools Are Not the Path

Letting go of attachment to tools, patterns, and dogma

If You Meet the Perfect Framework on the Road, Abandon It

Modern Koan: "The perfect framework is an illusion."
Original Koan: "If you meet the Buddha on the road, kill him."

Naming Things is Hard Because Thinking is Hard

Modern Koan: "He who names well, sees clearly."
Original Koan: "What is the name of the soundless bell?"

You Modernize Their Code. I Modernize Their Understanding.

Modern Koan: "The system is not the code. It is the thinking behind it."
Original Koan: "What was your original face before your parents were born?"

Every Tool Introduces a New Kind of Pain

Modern Koan: "Each solution brings a new problem. Choose wisely."
Original Koan: "How do you step off a hundred-foot pole?"

A Pattern is Not a Practice

Modern Koan: "Patterns don't solve problems. Practice does."
Original Koan: "What is the sound of practice without intention?" (an abstraction, not canonical)

Part III: Leadership Without Control

Mentorship, presence, and ego-free leadership

Guide Without Gripping

Modern Koan: "To lead is not to hold. It is to open the path."
Original Koan: "The wild geese do not intend to cast their reflection; the water has no mind to receive their image."

Code Review is a Conversation, Not a Performance

Modern Koan: "If the review is loud, the learning is silent."
Original Koan: "When you speak, you only repeat what you already know."

Strong Opinions, Loosely Held — Until Tested

Modern Koan: "Attachment to belief is the first bug."
Original Koan: "Does a dog have Buddha nature?" (Answer: "Mu")

Leadership is Naming the Problem No One Wants to Say

Modern Koan: "The silent bug crashes the system."
Original Koan: "When nothing is said, everything is heard." (paraphrased Zen theme)

Mentorship is Debugging the Mind, Not Just the Code

Modern Koan: "To fix the bug, first calm the panic."
Original Koan: "When the mind is disturbed, is it the wind or the flag that moves?"

Part IV: The Self in the System

Ego, identity, impermanence, and detachment

Your Career is Not Your Codebase

Modern Koan: "You are not your pull request."
Original Koan: "No self, no problem."

Ego Writes Fragile Code

Modern Koan: "When the coder disappears, the code strengthens."
Original Koan: "Emptiness is form, form is emptiness."

Like All Things, This Too Changes

Modern Koan: "Every system is temporary. Every title fades."
Original Koan: "All compounded things are impermanent."

Let Go or Be Dragged

Modern Koan: "Holding too tightly invites the crash."
Original Koan: "The tighter you grasp, the more you lose."

The Job is Temporary. The Impact Might Not Be.

Modern Koan: "You won't be here forever. The next coder will."
Original Koan: "A single spark can light ten thousand lamps."

Part V: Practices for the Mindful Developer

Habits that encourage awareness, clarity, and sustainability

Start with Stillness (Again)

Modern Koan: "Breathe before you build."
Original Koan: "The quieter you become, the more you hear."

Walk the Code Once Before You Fix It

Modern Koan: "Read before you rewrite. Listen before you speak."
Original Koan: "Step by step in the dark — if you don't look for the light, you may become it."

Make Commit Messages a Journal of Intent

Modern Koan: "Say what you meant. Not just what you did."
Original Koan: "Right speech arises from right intention."

Practice Deleting More Than You Add

Modern Koan: "The clearest code is the code that is gone."
Original Koan: "A cup is useful because of its emptiness."

Close the Laptop With Intention

Modern Koan: "When the workday ends, let it end."
Original Koan: "When you're walking, just walk. When you're sitting, just sit."

Beyond the Commit – Glossary of Terms

Abstraction

A way of hiding complexity in code by creating simplified interfaces or layers. Like using a light switch instead of wiring the electricity yourself.

Agile

A flexible approach to software development focused on iterative progress, collaboration, and responsiveness to change. Often misused as a buzzword, but still valuable when practiced with intention.

API (Application Programming Interface)

A set of rules that allow one piece of software to talk to another. Think of it as a restaurant menu—your app places an order, the kitchen (API) handles the request.

Architecture (Software)

The high-level structure of a software system. It's not just how things are built—it's how they're organized, how they interact, and where the seams are.

Bitmasking

A technique for storing multiple yes/no (binary) values in a single number using bits. Clever, compact, and occasionally cryptic.

Bounded Context

A design principle from Domain-Driven Design. It means defining clear boundaries around what concepts mean within a given part of a system—so one "user" doesn't mean five different things in five different places.

Cargo Cult Programming

Blindly copying patterns or practices without understanding why they're used. It looks like ritual, but lacks clarity or intention.

CI/CD (Continuous Integration / Continuous Deployment)

Automation practices for testing and delivering code. CI catches bugs early. CD helps push updates frequently and safely.

Code Review

A collaborative process where developers examine each other's code changes. Ideally a conversation—not a performance.

Cognitive Bloat

Mental overload caused by clinging to certainty or over-complicating systems. The software equivalent of trying to juggle flaming swords and deadlines at once.

Commit

A saved change in version control. It's like writing a journal entry in the history of your codebase.

Diff

Short for "difference." Shows what changed between two versions of a file or codebase.

Event Bus

A system where different parts of software can communicate through events, like passing messages on a shared channel. Useful—but easy to overengineer.

Framework

A pre-built foundation for building applications. Helps reduce boilerplate code, but often comes with tradeoffs and assumptions.

Git

A version control system used by developers to track changes in code over time. Like time travel for your code.

Imposter Syndrome

The persistent feeling that you don't belong or aren't good enough—despite evidence to the contrary. Common in tech, rarely accurate.

Interface

In code, an interface defines a contract: "Here's what this thing can do." It doesn't say how—just what's expected.

Koan

A paradoxical statement or question used in Zen Buddhism to provoke insight or challenge assumptions. In this book, adapted as a reflective anchor for each chapter.

Linter

A tool that analyzes code for potential errors or style violations. Like a grammar checker, but for programming.

Microservice

A small, self-contained piece of an application that handles one part of the system. Often used to build flexible, scalable systems—but can easily multiply complexity.

ORM (Object-Relational Mapping)

A tool that lets you interact with a database using objects in your code instead of raw SQL queries. Helpful—until it leaks.

Pattern (Design Pattern)

A reusable solution to a common coding problem. Like a blueprint—but one you still have to adapt to the actual terrain.

Refactor

Improving the structure of code without changing its behavior. Kind of like reorganizing your garage without throwing anything away (yet).

Repository (Repo)

A place where your code lives—tracked, versioned, and shared with your team.

Semantic Satiation

When a word is repeated so much it temporarily loses meaning. Happens a lot with overused names like "manager" or "service."

Sprint

A short, focused period (often 1–2 weeks) in agile development where a team commits to delivering specific work. Can feel like a focused effort—or a treadmill.

Stack

The technologies used to build an application (e.g., frontend, backend, database). A "tech stack" is like the ingredient list for your software.

Syntax

The rules that define how code must be written in a given language. Kind of like grammar in spoken language.

Technical Debt

The accumulated cost of shortcuts, old decisions, or missing improvements in code. It builds interest the longer it's ignored.

About the Author

Michael Payne is a veteran software developer, consultant, and founder of coexius, where he helps businesses modernize their systems with clarity and compassion. With over 25 years of experience across industries—from trucking and healthcare to federal government and finance—he's seen how code shapes teams, cultures, and lives.

A lifelong student of both technology and mindfulness, Michael writes and mentors at the intersection of software craft and personal growth. His unique approach blends technical depth with a calm, reflective perspective, encouraging developers to build systems—and careers—that are resilient, sustainable, and human-centered.

Michael lives in Texas with his wife, daughter, and three sons, where he spends his time thinking deeply about code, leadership, and the messy beauty of being human. When he's not working, you can find him exploring new frameworks, practicing presence, or revisiting *Star Trek* and *Star Wars* for timeless wisdom.

You can connect with me on:

🌐 https://www.coexius.com

🔗 https://www.linkedin.com/in/mepjr